MAY 2016

A Kid's Guide to

Keystone
Species
in Nature

Keystone Species that Live in Ponds, Streams, & Wetlands

BONNIE HINMAN

Mitchell Lane
PUBLISHERS
P.O. Box 196
Hockessin, DE 19707
www.mitchelllane.com

Mitchell Lane
PUBLISHERS

Printing   1   2   3   4   5   6   7   8

Keystone Species that Live in Deserts
Keystone Species that Live in Forests
Keystone Species that Live in Grasslands
Keystone Species that Live in the Mountains
Keystone Species that Live in Ponds, Streams, and Wetlands
Keystone Species that Live in the Sea and Along the Coastline

Library of Congress Cataloging-in-Publication Data
Hinman, Bonnie.
 Keystone species that live in ponds, streams, and wetlands / by Bonnie Hinman.
    pages cm. — (A kid's guide to keystone species in nature)
Includes bibliographical references and index.
Audience: Ages 8 to 11.
Audience: Grades 3 to 6.
ISBN 978-1-68020-062-1 (library bound)
1. Keystone species—Juvenile literature. 2. Freshwater ecology—Juvenile literature. 3. Freshwater animals—Juvenile literature. I. Title.
QH541.15.K48H558 2015
577.2'6—dc23
                                                                    2015005673
eBook ISBN: 978-1-68020-063-8

Contents

Words in **bold** throughout can be found in the Glossary.

Introduction

Most arches built today contain a single building block at the top that is the most important piece. This special piece can be found in the arches of soaring cathedrals, doorways in temples, and even simple buildings made out of wooden blocks. It is called a keystone, and it holds everything else together. Remove the keystone and the building or doorway is likely to collapse.

The same thing is true in nature. Certain species of animals and plants are so important to their **ecosystems**, that if they disappear, the whole system may collapse. They are called keystone species.

Some keystone species are large, like American alligators, while others are small, like freshwater crayfish. But size doesn't matter in an ecosystem. All living things

A keystone of a palace archway

Mealtime for a North American beaver

rely on other species to survive. A keystone species plays an especially large role that affects many different species in an ecosystem. Some keystone species are at the top of a huge ecosystem like the Greater Yellowstone Ecosystem, while others may affect a tiny ecosystem in a river or forest. Whether the ecosystem is big or small, the result of a keystone species disappearing or being greatly reduced is the same. Just like one falling domino can cause many others to fall, the loss of a keystone species can lead to the extinction of many other species.

Today scientists are focusing more attention on preserving the natural balance in ecosystems. Identifying and protecting keystone species is an important part of their work.

Chapter 1

AMERICAN ALLIGATOR

"See you later, alligator!" "In a while, crocodile!" Kids have been reciting this rhyme for many years. But by the time kids began shouting these words, alligators and crocodiles had already been around for millions of years.

Crocodiles and alligators can be difficult to tell apart, which is not surprising—they are related. Both animals belong to an **order** of reptiles called crocodilians. There are twenty-three different species of crocodilians in the world. Two are **native** to the United States. One is called the American alligator and the other is called the American crocodile. Although the two species have the same general shape, their **snouts** are different and so are their teeth.

American alligators almost became extinct in the twentieth century. The skin on an alligator's belly makes nice leather for shoes, handbags, belts, and other accessories. As many as ten million alligators were killed for their skins before 1970.[1] Fortunately, the US Fish and Wildlife Service and state wildlife agencies worked together to stop alligator hunting in the early 1970s. Alligator populations quickly recovered, and they are not endangered today.

This adult American alligator relaxes in a grassy spot in a wetland. Alligators are the largest reptiles in North America. Like many other reptiles, they warm their bodies by leaving the water to lay out in the sun.

An American alligator is an **apex predator**. Once an alligator has grown to about 4 feet (1.2 meters) long, it has no predators other than man. An alligator's thick skin has bony plates called scutes (SKYOOTZ). These scutes along with sharp teeth and a strong tail protect adult alligators from just about any animal that might want to attack them.

Homes and Bodies

American alligators live in the southeastern United States. They can be found as far north as North Carolina, and as far west as the Rio Grande river in Texas. They make their homes in swamps, marshes, rivers, and lakes. They seem to like calm waters, probably because it is easier for them to swim with their noses just above the water. Unlike American crocodiles, who can live in saltwater or freshwater, American alligators prefer to live in freshwater.

Male American alligators are usually about 13 or 14 feet (4 to 4.5 meters) long, while females are 9 or

Where American Alligators Are Found

LEGEND

◾ Area where American alligators naturally live

◾ Areas where nonnative alligators have been found

10 feet (3 meters) long. Occasionally alligators can grow to 20 feet (6 meters) or longer. Adults usually weigh about 330 pounds (150 kilograms),[2] but the largest males can weigh up to 1,000 pounds (450 kilograms).[3]

Both male and female alligators are brown or black with creamy white bellies. Their legs are short, but they can still run quickly on land. Alligators have a rounded snout and may have up to eighty teeth at a time. As their teeth wear down and fall out, new ones grow in. An alligator could have as many as three thousand teeth in its lifetime.[4]

Young Alligators and Alligator Meals

Alligators are ready to breed when they are six or seven feet (two meters) long, rather than at a certain age. Usually alligators are eight to fifteen years old when they reach this size. Males grow to this length sooner than females do.

Alligators breed at night. The male roars or bellows and sometimes raises his head out of the water. Both the male and female call to each other and blow bubbles underwater. They may try to push one another underwater. This is an attempt by each one to see how strong the other is.

Breeding takes place in April and May. The female builds a mounded nest of mud, leaves, and other vegetation. She lays twenty-five to sixty eggs[5] in late June or early July. The female then covers the eggs with more mud and leaves, and stays near the nests while the eggs **incubate** for about nine weeks. She is very protective and she will attack if the nest is threatened.

The temperature determines whether the alligator babies will be male or female. If the eggs incubate at 90 to 93°F (32 to 34°C), the baby alligators will become males. Eggs incubating at 82 to 86°F (28 to 30°C) will become females. Temperatures in the middle produce a mix of males and females.[6]

When the eggs are ready to hatch in August or September, the babies inside the eggs make a high-pitched noise. This sound alerts the mother alligator that her babies are hatching. She removes the top of the nest, and then carries the newly hatched babies in her mouth or on her back to the nearby water. The mother will defend her tiny hatchlings for the first year and sometimes longer. The father alligators do not help the mothers take care of the babies.

The little alligators are from six to ten inches (fifteen to twenty-five centimeters) long when they hatch. They grow rapidly at a rate of one foot (thirty centimeters) a year until they are around five years old. Young alligators live in small groups called pods. Life is dangerous for a baby alligator. Herons, snakes, raccoons, and older alligators like to snack on them. Less than 9 percent of the hatchlings will survive to become adults,[7] even though the mother tries to protect them.

American alligators can live as long as fifty years in the wild and sixty-five to eighty years in captivity.[8] Young alligators eat insects and small **invertebrates**. As they get older they eat bigger prey, including mammals, fish, turtles, and birds. Adults will eat almost anything including cans, bottles, nails, and even rocks. Scientists think that since alligators don't chew their food, these objects help break down food inside the stomach.

A pod of young American alligators stick together in Okefenokee Swamp. This wetland is located in southern Georgia and northern Florida. The young alligators' yellow stripes will fade as the reptiles get older.

Needed in the Wetlands

Alligators affect their environments in several ways. One of those ways is by eating species of fish that can overpopulate a wetland. Gars are a good example of fish that can take over a wetland if they do not have predators. Gars are large fish, and they eat a large number of other smaller fish. If there are too many gars in an area, soon there will be no fish but gars. Alligators keep the number of gars under control and allow the other fish to thrive.

In wetlands like the Everglades in Florida, the land is flooded during the rainy season. In the winter dry season, however, the water level drops and the land is dry. Alligators dig holes which hold water even when the higher ground nearby dries out. These holes become ponds which are sources of water for snakes, turtles, birds, and other animals during the dry season. Insect **larvae**, tadpoles, and small fish also live in these holes.

These tiny species are food for birds and snakes. Without alligator holes, many animals would die or leave the wetlands during the dry season. But with these holes, lots of animals can remain there all year round. When the wet season returns, the animals move out of the alligator holes and across the wetlands. By digging these holes, alligators help keep the wetlands food chain alive.[9]

People are often afraid of alligators. These reptiles almost never attack humans, but it does happen. Scientists think that many attacks happen after people have fed alligators. This causes the alligators to lose their fear of people and to see them as a source of food. A female may also attack if she has to defend her nest.

Alligators do have trouble finding food sometimes because their **habitats** have been destroyed. People have drained wetlands in order to build homes, stores, and roads. This has forced alligators to live in smaller and smaller areas.

American alligators and people can live peacefully together as long as we give each other plenty of space. That means that people will have to stop building in their habitat. And never, ever feed an alligator.

In Florida, people have drained wetlands and built their homes on land that was once only used by alligators and other wild animals. Because of this, alligators and humans are living closer together than ever before. This sign warns residents to watch out for alligators in this waterway that crosses through their neighborhood.

Is It an Alligator
or a Crocodile?

Teeth tell the story when you are trying to figure out if the large, scaly reptile you see is an alligator or crocodile. If you can see at least one large pointed tooth on each side when the mouth is closed, it's a crocodile. If only small or no teeth show, it's an alligator.[10] A crocodile's skin is lighter and his snout is more pointed than an alligator's. Their **ranges** overlap but most crocodiles live further south than alligators. American crocodiles are endangered. American alligators are not endangered any longer, but they are still listed as threatened because hunters may confuse the two reptiles.

American alligator

American crocodile

Chapter 2

FRESHWATER CRAYFISH

Crayfish are often seen darting around the shallows of a creek, looking a bit like tiny lobsters. In some parts of the United States, they are called crawdads or crawfish. Some people call them crawcrabs or mudbugs. No matter what you call them, they are all crayfish.

In spite of their name, crayfish are **crustaceans** rather than fish. There are more than 640 species of crayfish in the world. Scientists find new species every year. They live in many areas, including North America, South America, Europe, Asia, and Australia. The southeastern United States and southeastern Australia have more species than any other part of the world.[1]

Crayfish have been on Earth for a long time. Fossil records suggest that they were here 286 million years ago.[2] People have been eating crayfish for a long time, too. Pieces of crayfish shells have been found in twenty-eight-thousand-year-old cooking hearths in Australia. Crayfish were not widely eaten in Europe until the Middle Ages, when they became popular in France and England. By the sixteenth century, crayfish dishes were being eaten by wealthy Germans and Scandinavians.[3] Today crayfish are

A colorful yabby crayfish is peeking out of the water in Mulyangarie Station, Australia. Crayfish have gills and breathe underwater. However, they can live on land for several days as long as their gills remain wet.

This savory dish of crayfish and potatoes is the main course at a crayfish boil party. Crayfish boil parties are often held outside since they are a little messy. The crayfish are boiled in a big pot along with vegetables and seasonings.

a popular food in the southeastern United States. They are often boiled and used in soups and stews.

Life in the Water

Crayfish have rigid **exoskeletons** that are a lot like suits of armor. They can still move freely because the exoskeleton divides into sections that have flexible joints. The front part of a crayfish's body is called the cephalothorax (sef-uh-loh-THAWR-aks) and the back part is the abdomen (AB-duh-muhn). Crayfish have eight walking legs and two pincers (PIN-serz) or claws. They have gills for breathing in water like fish do.

Most of the time crayfish walk along the bottom of a stream or lake using their legs while holding their pincers up in front. If something scares a crayfish, it will curl its tail under its body. It jerks the tail forward, causing its body to dart backward.[4] Sometimes this unexpected movement startles a predator enough that the crayfish can escape.

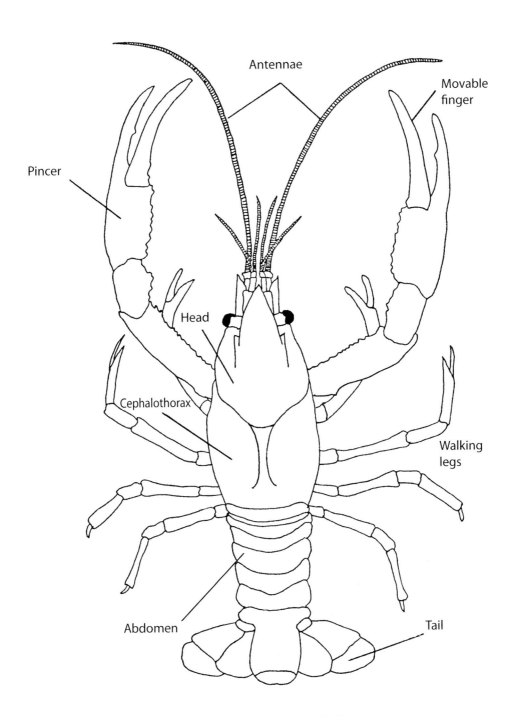

Antennae

Movable finger

Pincer

Head

Cephalothorax

Walking legs

Abdomen

Tail

Anatomy of a Crayfish

Crayfish mate at different times of the year depending on the species. Sometimes a female keeps her eggs for many months before releasing them. When the female is ready to release her eggs, she pushes them into a sac on the underside of her abdomen. She attaches the eggs to small abdominal limbs called swimmerets (SWIM-uh-rets), where they will incubate on her body.

When the eggs hatch, the babies remain attached to their mother's swimmerets.[5] They stay this way for several weeks before breaking free to swim alone. However, even after breaking free, the tiny crayfish return to attach themselves onto her abdomen if they feel threatened.

Molting

Because they have a rigid exoskeleton, crayfish cannot grow like other animals. They must molt, which they begin doing while still attached to their mother. A new slightly larger exoskeleton develops under the old one.

When the new skeleton is ready, the old shell splits open. Out pops the crayfish wearing a new shell. This new shell is very soft for the first few days. A soft crayfish makes a tasty meal for a predator and sometimes even for another crayfish. Usually a crayfish hides under rocks or in other protected places during molting.

Scientists believe that molting is **stressful** to crayfish. Sometimes they die after leaving their old shell. Occasionally molting goes wrong and a claw or leg remains behind in the old shell. Crayfish are able to regrow these missing parts in a process called regeneration. However, the new claws or legs are seldom the same size or shape as the old ones.

Young crayfish molt several times during their first months of life. They usually molt only two to five times in their second year. Different species of crayfish have different life spans, but on average they live between one and three years.[6] Most adult crayfish will be between one and five inches (three to thirteen centimeters) in length, depending on the species.

A Delicate Balance

Crayfish live under rocks and logs at the bottoms of lakes, ponds, rivers, and streams. They are omnivorous (om-NIV-er-uhs) meaning that they will eat plants or animals.[7] In fact, crayfish will eat just about anything that they can get in their mouths. They eat dead plants and animals as well as live plants, invertebrates, fish eggs, and small fish.

Crayfish are a major prey species in their environments. More than two hundred different species of fish, amphibians, reptiles, birds, and mammals eat crayfish.[8] This alone makes crayfish a keystone species. Because so many other animals depend on crayfish for their food, it would be disastrous for the crayfish to disappear. If that happened, many other species in that same habitat might die or move away.

Some crayfish also burrow into stream banks, wetlands, and even lawns. When crayfish dig their burrows or holes, they bring nutrient-rich underground soil to the surface, which keeps their ecosystems healthy. These burrows also provide hiding places for frogs, snakes, rodents, and fish.

Crayfish do cause problems sometimes. When a nonnative crayfish is turned loose in an area, it can eat native fish, amphibians, other crayfish, and plants.

In some cases the newcomer **competes** with the native crayfish for food and shelter and can quickly take over a habitat. In this case, it is called an invasive species. This crayfish helped keep the ecosystem in balance in its original habitat, but it destroys the balance in the new one.

Invasive crayfish are hard to get rid of. The best way to deal with invasive crayfish is to keep them from getting into nonnative habitats in the first place. It is usually people who introduce crayfish to a new environment. Fishermen who use crayfish as bait sometimes release unused live crayfish into a stream or lake. This purchased bait may not be a native species.

Crayfish may escape from aquariums or be released on purpose from schools where they have been used for science education.[9] It is possible to purchase crayfish from a pet store or online. These crayfish are seldom native to the areas they are sent to, so they become invasive if released.

Even though there are hundreds of species of crayfish in the world, many are endangered. In addition to the threats posed by invasive crayfish, human land use causes problems for native crayfish. As land is disturbed for construction or farming, **sediment** can collect at the bottom of nearby streams. This sediment fills up the space between rocks and logs and the bottom of the stream, making it harder for crayfish to burrow underneath.[10]

You can do your part to help by never moving crayfish from one place to another. Also, do not release your fishing bait or turn your pet crayfish loose outside. We need these funny-looking creatures to maintain the natural balance in our world.

The Tasmanian Giant Freshwater Crayfish

If you jump when a three-inch long crayfish nibbles at your toes in the creek, you would move even faster if you saw a Tasmanian (taz-MEY-nee-uhn) giant freshwater crayfish. These jumbo-sized crayfish are the largest freshwater invertebrates in the world. They live in Tasmania, Australia. The Tasmanian giant freshwater crayfish can live for forty years, grow to over three feet (one meter) long, and weigh up to thirteen pounds (six kilograms). They do not become adults until they are nine to fourteen years old.[11] Females only have babies every other year. This species is threatened because humans have been taking over its habitat and **poaching** it for food. This is especially hard on these crustaceans because it takes them so long to reproduce.

Chapter 3

NORTH AMERICAN BEAVER

"**Y**ou're just as busy as a beaver!" Has anyone ever said that to you? If so, you were probably very busy, because beavers are among the hardest workers in the animal kingdom. The business of a beaver is clear to him or her: cut down trees, build a dam to create a pond, build a lodge, and store food at the bottom of the pond. No beaver rests for long until everything is prepared for winter.

There are two species of beavers. The North American beaver lives throughout most of Canada and the United States, and in the northern parts of Mexico. The Eurasian beaver lives in parts of Europe and northern Asia. Both species neared extinction from hunting but both are slowly recovering their numbers.

Beavers are wetlands **engineers** because they change the land and water around them. They build dams and dig channels in just a few weeks. This can help other animals in the ecosystem, but it can also cause some problems for humans. When a beaver dams up a stream, the pond created can be a home for many other species. But a beaver's dam can also cause farmland, roads, or buildings

When this North American beaver dives into the pond, he closes valves in his ears and nose to keep out the water. He also has eye membranes that act as swim goggles. A beaver's large hind feet are webbed and allow him to swim much faster than he can walk on land.

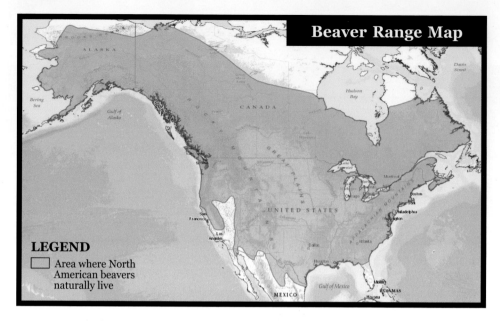

Beaver Range Map

LEGEND

☐ Area where North American beavers naturally live

to flood. That is not a good result for the people who live or work on the land or use it to grow food.

The beaver is the second-largest rodent in the world. Only the South American capybara is bigger. Adult North American beavers usually weigh between forty and sixty pounds (eighteen and twenty-seven kilograms). They grow up to about 50 inches (130 centimeters) long including their tails. The tail alone can be up to eighteen inches (forty-six centimeters) long and seven inches (eighteen centimeters) wide.

Tails, Fur, and Teeth

A beaver's long, flat tail is used in many ways. It stores fat that the beaver's body needs during long winters. Beavers also use their tails to steer when they swim. They lean back against them for balance when they stand on their hind legs. A beaver may also fold its tail underneath itself like a chair when it sits down to groom itself.

Some people think that beavers use their tails to carry mud to build dams. Instead, they use their front paws like hands to move mud and pat it into place on a dam. Although a beaver slaps its tail on the water to warn of danger, it fights enemies with its teeth and claws.

Beavers have brown fur that they **waterproof** by coating it with castoreum (ka-STAWR-ee-uhm). They produce this oily liquid in **glands** located near the base of their tails. Beavers spend a lot of time grooming themselves. Their beautiful thick fur almost caused them to disappear from the earth completely. Throughout history hunters killed large numbers of them to make hats and coats.

A beaver's teeth never stop growing. Orange in color, these teeth wear down as the beaver gnaws away at trees. The front teeth are sharpened as they wear down. They use the sharp edges of their front teeth to cut down trees in minutes. A beaver can bring down a tree with a six-inch (fifteen-centimeter) **diameter** in less than fifty minutes.[1]

Eurasian and North American beavers look alike in many ways. This Eurasian beaver shows off his orange teeth that look just like a North American beaver's front teeth. However, the two kinds of beavers are different species and they cannot interbreed.

Getting to Work

Adult beaver couples arrive in a new area with a plan. They know what to do and waste no time getting started. They need a stream and prefer slower running water. Aspen, birch, poplar, and willow are some of their favorite foods, so they choose an area with plenty of these trees nearby. They will eat the twigs, leaves, and bark, and use the hard inner wood for building materials.

First beavers build a dam to make the stream or river deeper. Deep water is safer for young beavers. They can dive underwater quickly to escape predators like wolves, bears, and coyotes. Males and females both cut down trees and pull them to the stream. They use logs, branches, and stones to make the dam and plaster everything together with mud.

As the dam is built higher, the water behind the dam gets deeper. The surrounding land is flooded and a pond forms. The beavers check for leaks by listening for escaping water, and they are quick to fix any leaks they find. Most dams are less than one hundred feet (thirty meters) long but much longer ones have been recorded.[2]

Next it is time to build a house. A lodge is built the same way a dam is, with sticks and branches, but it is usually in the middle of the new pond. The lodge's floor is above the water, and it contains two or more "rooms." The only entrance to the lodge is under the water. Beavers dive down into the pond and surface through an opening in the floor of their lodge.

If winter is coming, the next step for beavers is to build an underwater food **cache**. They cut even more trees and store the branches on the pond's bottom in case ice covers the surface of the pond in winter. If this happens,

Inside look at a beaver lodge.

the beavers could be trapped under the ice, only able to reach their lodges by the underwater opening. The cache leaves food within reach on the pond's bottom.

Beaver Families

Beavers mate once a year, sometime between December and March. Their babies are called kits and are born between April and June. There are usually three or four kits in a **litter**. They have all their fur and teeth at birth. Within an hour, they are exploring the lodge and learning to swim.

The kits will nurse for the first few weeks or months. When they are a few days or weeks old, their parents will start bringing grasses and other plants into the lodge for them to eat. Even after the kits are **weaned** and able to swim around the pond, their parents still provide them with food. The older siblings help the parents take care of the kits. The kits do not leave to make a home for themselves until they are about two years old, and some stay longer.

Engineering an Ecosystem

Beavers are important to their habitats for many reasons. They create and maintain wetlands that are home to numerous species. Dams slow water movement in a stream. Some species do not like the fast-moving water in a stream. These species would not live in the area if the beaver pond did not exist.

Beavers also cause different trees to grow around their ponds. When they cut down their favorites, other trees have less competition. These trees attract different kinds of birds and insects. Habitats with lots of different animals and plants are healthier and likely to stay that way. Scientists call this mixture of plants and animals biodiversity.

When food sources run out, the beaver family moves out of its lodge and pond. But they still help other species after they are gone. The untended dam breaks, allowing the pond to drain. The bottom of the pond becomes dry land with rich soil, called a "beaver meadow." The meadow can then become home to many other species that could not live in the nearby forest. Once plants and trees have regrown, beavers may return to the area once again.

While beavers benefit their ecosystem greatly, many people see them as pests. They might cause flooding in farms, parks, golf courses, or backyards. Trees that people have planted to make their yard more beautiful might look more like dinner to a beaver. Because of this, people still try to get rid of beavers. If we can learn to live with them instead, it will be a small price to pay to keep these wetlands engineers around to help balance our natural world.

Skydiving Beavers

In the 1940s, people began moving onto land in Idaho where beavers lived. This caused problems for the people and the beavers, so the Idaho Fish and Game Department planned to move the beavers to areas where they would be far from human homes and businesses. At first, they tried moving beavers by truck and by horse or mule. The long, rough trip was hard on the beavers, and many of them died. So in 1948 the Idaho Fish and Game Department tried a new way to move the beavers. They put pairs of beavers in crates and loaded them on airplanes. The planes dropped the crates by parachute in different locations. When the crates hit the ground, they opened. Only one beaver died in the fall. The other seventy-five immediately began building dams and raising kits.

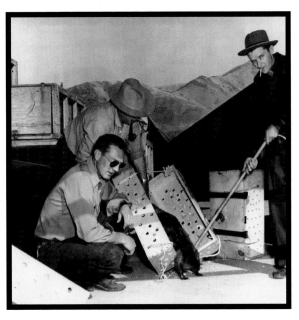

Chapter 4
EASTERN NEWT

A newt looks a little like a lizard but is a very different kind of animal. Eastern newts and all other newts are amphibians, while lizards are reptiles. An amphibian always lives part of its life in water and part of its life on land. It doesn't have scales like a reptile does. Frogs are amphibians, for example, and their tadpoles live in water after hatching. Eventually they grow legs and become land creatures. Newts are one of the amphibians in the salamander family. They live part of their lives in water, too.

Salamanders have been around for at least 150 million years. These ancient animals live in forests, wetlands, streams, and ponds. The eastern newt is one of more than six hundred species of salamanders.[1] They live from Canada in the north to Texas, Alabama, Georgia, and Florida in the southern United States. Eastern newts have four subspecies: the broken-striped newt, the central newt, the peninsula newt, and the red-spotted newt.

The Life of an Eastern Newt

Eastern newts have four stages of development. They begin as eggs which hatch in the water. The hatchlings are called larvae. After a few months as a larva, the newt

This eastern newt has transformed into its eft stage. It searches for insects on a dead log in Allegany State Park in New York State.

Eastern Newt Range Map

LEGEND

■ Area where eastern newts naturally live

usually changes into an eft. The larva's gills disappear and it grows legs. The eft leaves the water to live on land. After several years, the eft changes again and goes back to the water to live as an adult eastern newt.

Newt eggs are laid in late spring and hatch after a three to eight week incubation period. The larvae are less than half an inch (thirteen millimeters) long when they hatch. These tiny creatures have flat, pointed tails, gray, green, or brown skin, and gills. The hatchlings grow quickly and are one to two inches (three to five centimeters) long when they **metamorphose** to the eft stage several months later.

The larvae eat tiny invertebrates and other larvae. They stay mostly on the muddy bottom of the pond. They do not move around much because that would attract the attention of predators. Predators include the much larger adult newts who don't mind eating their own kind. Few newt larvae manage to live long enough to transform into the eft stage.

Larvae usually change into efts after two to five months. In warmer climates larvae sometimes skip this stage and become adults without ever leaving the water. The larvae that do become efts lose their gills and grow lungs. Their two-chambered hearts transform into three-chambered hearts. The eft has reddish-orange skin with a yellow-orange belly. On its back are red spots surrounded by black circles. The bright colors warn predators to stay away. An eft is poisonous to some predators and just tastes terrible to others.

Scientists have discovered that larvae form a group in the pond shortly before moving onto land. The newly formed efts usually crawl out of the water at night or when it has just stopped raining. They migrate in waves into the nearby forest. Once in the forest they search for food in the dead leaves under trees. Their favorite foods include snails, worms, and insects. A few predators do eat efts in spite of their warning color.

Efts remain on the forest floor for two to seven years. As the efts transform into their adult form, they move back to the water. Their color changes to greenish brown but they keep their spots. Adults are three to five inches (seven to twelve centimeters) long, and they have slightly moist skin. Their eyes are small with a slit **pupil**.

Adult newts live in and near the water. If their ponds dry up, they can survive on land, but will only lay eggs in water. Adults are not picky eaters. They will eat any small invertebrate that comes their way, but they especially love insects.

Many predators stay away from the adults even though the adults' skin is not as poisonous as the efts'. Still, smallmouth bass, snakes, and raccoons eat adult eastern newts.

Breeding takes place once a year, in the late winter or early spring. The female lays two hundred to four hundred eggs over several weeks.[2] Each egg is laid separately on an underwater plant. Sometimes she only lays a few eggs a day. Once egg laying is done, the female swims away. Eastern newt parents do not play any part in raising their babies.

Keystone Predators

Eastern newts are common throughout the eastern United States. But they need ponds and other wetlands to survive. Wetlands are often drained for construction and forests or woodlands are reduced for the same purpose. If this continues, their numbers could eventually decrease.

Eastern newts are keystone predators, which means that they are important to their habitat because of the other species that they eat. This is especially true in ponds that sometimes dry out and refill. Eastern newts can continue to live in the mud of a dried out pond until the water returns. They are often the first species living in the pond when it does refill. If they were not around, a few species would quickly take over the pond and no other species could live there. The ecosystem would be out of balance. However the newts eat many of these species and their eggs, which leaves room for a greater number of species to establish populations in the pond.

Eastern newts also help protect humans from mosquito bites. Mosquito eggs are among their favorite foods. So wherever eastern newts are found, there will be fewer mosquitoes.

The ways that eastern newts affect their environments help keep many other animals living nearby. As with other keystone species, the loss of the eastern newts would change the balance required for a healthy ecosystem. It is important for many species that we protect their habitat in the future.

Where Do They Get Those Long Names?

Sometimes when we study an animal or plant, we discover that it has a long funny-looking name as well as the common one. A scientist may call a broken-striped newt by another name: *Notophtalmus viridescens dorsalis*. In 1757, scientist Carl Linnaeus invented a classification system to name plants and animals. He used Latin as the language of his system. All living creatures are divided into classes or groups. Three domains are at the top of the chart. Domains are further divided into six kingdoms. Humans are in the Animalia kingdom just like dogs and salamanders. The kingdoms are subdivided several more times. The scientific name is made up of the final three divisions: the genus, the species, and the subspecies. Modern humans have the scientific name *Homo sapiens sapiens*.

Carl Linnaeus

Chapter 5

CHINOOK SALMON

Have you ever seen a fish climb a ladder? Some species of fish do climb ladders, but they are not the kind of ladders we usually see. Sometimes a dam or other barrier will block a stream, leaving salmon unable to pass. So people created fish ladders to help fish to get around these barriers. There are different kinds of fish ladders. Salmon like to use a ladder that has a series of small pools of water. The pools are built at the side of a dam and go up like a stairway. A salmon is a strong jumper. When the salmon wants to swim upstream, it jumps from pool to pool, moving up and over the dam.

Salmon are anadromous (uh-NAD-ruh-muhs) fish, meaning that they are born in fresh water, migrate to the ocean, and eventually return to the fresh water river or stream where they were born. Salmon live in both the Atlantic and Pacific oceans. Chinook salmon are the largest of several species of salmon that live in the Pacific Northwest.

Chinook salmon average 3 feet (91 centimeters) long and about 30 pounds (14 kilograms). But a chinook salmon can grow to over 5 feet (152 centimeters) and weigh as much as 110 pounds (50 kilograms).[1] They are

These chinook salmon were born in this river and made a long journey out to live in the Pacific Ocean while they were still growing. Now they have returned to their original home. Since their bodies have already changed to adapt to salt water, they will soon die. But first, they will lay eggs which will produce the next generation of chinook salmon.

blue-green on their head and back with silver sides. Their tails, backs, and upper fins have black spots.

Alevins, Fry, and Smolts

Chinook salmon begin their lives as eggs in a nest called a redd, which their mother has dug out of the gravel at the stream's bottom. Chinook salmon eggs are laid in deep, fast-flowing water. The eggs hatch from 90 to 150 days after being laid. The tiny fish are called alevins (AL-uh-vuhns). During the alevin stage of growth, the fish are attached to the yolk sac of their eggs. They remain in the gravel until the yolk sac food is used up.

Eventually the baby salmon emerge from the gravel and feed on **plankton**.

At this stage, the young fish are called fry. As they grow they eat insects and other small invertebrates. They remain in the stream for a few months to two years. Then they begin their migration downstream toward the ocean. During this time, their bodies begin to change in preparation for life in salt water. This is the smolt stage of development.

Smolts spend some time in estuaries (ES-choo-er-eez) before they move on to the ocean. Estuaries form at the end of rivers or streams where fresh water mixes with the salt water of the ocean. It's a **transition** zone for the salmon.

Ocean Life and a Long Journey Home

The amount of time a chinook salmon spends in the estuary depends on its size. Large fish will move to the ocean quickly; small fish will need to grow a bit first. Once they move from the estuary into the open ocean, they eat herring, pilchard, and sandlance fish plus squid and crustaceans. They may stay close to the coast or they may travel far out into the Pacific.

The time that chinook salmon spend in the ocean varies by several years. Some may only stay in the ocean for a year or two before beginning the trip back upstream. Others may stay in the ocean up to seven or eight years. They grow quickly during the time they are in the ocean. Chinook salmon need to gain as much weight as possible before they begin their long migration back to freshwater to **spawn**. When it is time to leave the ocean, their bodies begin to change. The fish turn a reddish color and the males' noses gain a hooked shape. Salmon have an **instinct** that directs them to return to the freshwater stream or river where they were born.

A chinook who came from the Yukon River in Canada may swim as far as 2,000 miles (3,200 kilometers) in sixty days.[2] Salmon do not eat during their migration. They survive on stored body fat, so their health gets worse as they get closer to the end of their journey.

It is a struggle for salmon to reach their spawning stream. They must swim against the flow of the water, and dams and other manmade barriers block the rivers and streams along the way. **Conservationists** have built various fish ladders to help the salmon, but many still do not survive to lay eggs. Hungry bears and eagles are another obstacle for the salmon. These hunters won't pass up an opportunity to catch a tasty salmon as large numbers of them swim upstream.

Once they reach their destination, the females dig redds while the males stand guard. A single female deposits from three thousand to fourteen thousand eggs in her redd.[3] Then the male deposits his **sperm** in the nest to **fertilize** the eggs. Both parents protect the nest until they die, usually within twenty-five days. The parents are long dead when the eggs hatch.

Important to Many

Chinook salmon are important both for people and for the other animals in the salmon's ecosystems. Commercial and sport fishermen catch salmon to be eaten by people. Salmon contains several important vitamins as well as fats called omega-3 fatty acids. Many nutritionists believe that eating salmon once or twice a week can help keep human brains, hearts, and other organs healthy.

By the time the salmon are adults living in the ocean, not many predators can harm them. Still, some large predators like killer whales eat the salmon. The salmon are important predators themselves when they eat their favorite ocean foods of fish and squid.

During the salmon's time in fresh water, they provide food for even more species. Birds and fish feed on salmon eggs and baby salmon. Eagles, bears, mink, and otters feed on the salmon that have died naturally after spawning. One study found that at least 138 species benefit from salmon in their environments.[4]

The bears alone may drag thousands of dead salmon into the forest. The bears' leftovers decompose and enrich the soil. Other dead salmon get washed up onto the riverbanks by the flow of the water. Scientists found that healthier plants grew in the soil along riverbanks where dead salmon had rotted.[5]

Chinook salmon are endangered or threatened in many habitats in the Pacific Northwest. In some areas, fishermen are killing too many salmon. In other areas, dams and obstacles can cause the water to flow in a different direction or with less force. If the water is not moving quickly enough, the salmon will not continue their journey upstream. Crossing the dams themselves also poses a serious problem for migrating salmon. Even the best fish ladders cannot entirely solve that problem. In addition, streams have become polluted with pesticides and other chemicals from nearby farms and factories, threatening the health of the streams and the salmon. And a warming climate has caused increases in river temperatures, which can kill migrating salmon before they reach their destination.

Governments and conservation groups have invested billions of dollars to keep salmon alive and well. Some conservationists have tried catching salmon before spawning and bringing them to a hatchery to spawn. The eggs are incubated and hatched in the lab. Later, the young fish are placed in the original stream. Conservationists hoped that these hatcheries would help increase population sizes. So far, however, the hatchery-raised salmon are not as healthy as wild salmon, and they are less successful at reproducing.[6] Other conservationists help the salmon in more natural ways. They focus on keeping healthy streams healthy, or they try to get dams removed or changed so they do not block the streams.

Chinook salmon are important to humans and many species in aquatic habitats. However if people continue to change and pollute their habitat, we may only see these fish in history books. It will be up to us to keep their rivers and streams healthy so the salmon will be around for many years to come.

A Fishy GPS System

Scientists have long wondered how salmon find their way back to the stream where they were born. A salmon might swim thousands of miles in the open ocean before it migrates back to the inland stream where it hatched up to seven or eight years earlier. Scientists now think that salmon use the earth's **magnetic fields** to **navigate** the huge distances. It seems that they may have a magnetic map in their heads from birth. They inherit the map from their parents, just like you might have inherited your parents' hair or eye color. During migrations to and from the ocean, this map tells the salmon exactly which direction and how far to travel.[7]

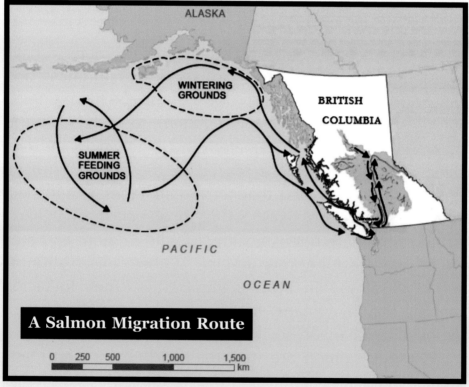

ALASKA

WINTERING
GROUNDS

BRITISH

COLUMBIA

SUMMER
FEEDING
GROUNDS

PACIFIC

OCEAN

A Salmon Migration Route

| 0 | 250 | 500 | 1,000 | 1,500 |
| | | | | km |

This map shows the migration route of a group of sockeye salmon that spawn in the Fraser River in British Columbia, Canada. Young smolts leave the spawning area and head out into the ocean, where they live for several years before they come back to the river to spawn and die.

CHAPTER NOTES

Chapter 1: American Alligator

1. Defenders of Wildlife, "American Alligator: Threats to American Alligators," http://www.defenders.org/american-alligator/threats

2. Lauren Pajerski, Benjamin Schechter, and Robin Street, *"Alligator mississippiensis,"* University of Michigan Museum of Zoology, *Animal Diversity Web*, October 4, 2000, http://animaldiversity.org/accounts/alligator_mississippiensis/

3. US Fish & Wildlife Service, "American Alligator: *Alligator mississippiensis*," February 2008, http://www.fws.gov/endangered/esa-library/pdf/alligator.pdf

4. New Hampshire Public Television, "American Alligator—*Alligator Mississippiensis*," *Nature Works*, http://www.nhptv.org/natureworks/americanalligator.htm

5. Cincinnati Zoo, "American Alligator," September 4, 2012, http://cincinnatizoo.org/wp-content/uploads/2013/03/American-Alligator-In-Progress.pdf

6. Pajerski, *"Alligator mississippiensis."*

7. Cincinnati Zoo, "American Alligator."

8. Pajerski, *"Alligator mississippiensis."*

9. US Fish & Wildlife Service, "American Alligator: *Alligator mississippiensis*."

10. National Park Service, "American Crocodile: Species Profile," Everglades National Park, http://www.nps.gov/ever/naturescience/crocodile.htm

Chapter 2: Freshwater Crayfish

1. Keith A. Crandall and Jennifer E. Buhay, "Global Diversity of Crayfish (Astacidae, Cambaridae, and Parastacidae—Decapoda) in Freshwater," *Hydrobiologia*, January 1, 2008, p. 295, http://decapoda.nhm.org/pdfs/27696/27696.pdf

2. Stephen T. Hasiotis, "Crayfish Fossils and Burrows from the Upper Triassic Chinle Formation, Canyonlands National Park, Utah," in Vincent L. Santucci and Lindsay McClelland, eds., *National Park Service Paleontological Research*, Volume 2 (Denver, CO: National Park Service, 1995), p. 78, http://www.nature.nps.gov/geology/paleontology/Publications/research_volumes/nps_paleo_vol2/research%20volume%202_paleo.pdf

3. F. Gherardi, "Towards a Sustainable Human Use of Freshwater Crayfish (Crustacea, Decapoda, Astacidea)," *Knowledge and Management of Aquatic Ecosystems*, issue 401, 2011, pp. 02p4, 02p6, http://www.kmae-journal.org/articles/kmae/pdf/2011/02/kmae110008.pdf

4. William L. Pflieger, *The Crayfishes of Missouri* (Jefferson City, MO: Missouri Department of Conservation, 1996), pp. 25–26.

5. Ibid., pp. 28–29.

6. Ibid., pp. 26–27.

7. Oregon Sea Grant, "Species at a Glance: Crayfish," *Aquatic Invasions! A Menace to the West*, http://seagrant.oregonstate.edu/sites/default/files/invasive-species/toolkit/crayfish.pdf

8. Daniel D. Magoulick, "Invasive Species Effects, Population Status and Population Genetics of Crayfish Species of Greatest Conservation Need (*Orconectes marchandi, Orconectes eupunctus,* and *Cambarus hubbsi*) in the Ozark Highlands of Arkansas and Missouri," Arkansas Wildlife Action Plan, 2014, http://www.wildlifearkansas.com/proposals/2014Preproposals/Preproposals2014.html

9. Oregon Sea Grant, "Crayfish Species at a Glance."

10. Zachary Loughman, "Crayfish," *e-WV: The West Virginia Encyclopedia*, August 1, 2014, http://www.wvencyclopedia.org/articles/2426

11. Parks & Wildlife Service, Tasmania, "Giant Freshwater Crayfish (*Astacopsis gouldi*)," November 28, 2011, http://www.parks.tas.gov.au/indeX.aspX?base=11213

Chapter 3: North American Beaver

1. Dietland Müller-Schwarze, *The Beaver: Its Life and Impact*, Second Edition (Ithaca, NY: Cornell University Press, 2011), p. 72.

2. Scott Jackson and Thomas Decker, "Beavers in Massachusetts," University of Massachusetts Cooperative Extension System, Massachusetts Division of Fisheries and Wildlife, http://www.bio.umass.edu/biology/conn.river/beaver.html

Chapter 4: Eastern Newt

1. AmphibiaWeb, "AmphibiaWeb Species Numbers," 2015, http://amphibiaweb.org/amphibian/speciesnums.html

2. Shannon Riemland, *"Notophthalmus viridescens*: Eastern Newt," University of Michigan Museum of Zoology, *Animal Diversity Web*, October 4, 2000, http://animaldiversity.org/accounts/Notophthalmus_viridescens/

Chapter 5: Chinook Salmon

1. National Wildlife Federation, "Chinook Salmon," http://nwf.org/wildlife/wildlife-library/amphibians-reptiles-and-fish/chinook-salmon.aspx

2. Kevin Delaney, "Chinook Salmon," Alaska Department of Fish & Game, 2008, http://www.adfg.alaska.gov/static/education/wns/chinook_salmon.pdf

3. Caren Scott, *"Oncorhynchus tshawytscha*: Blackmouth," University of Michigan Museum of Zoology, *Animal Diversity Web*, June 2, 2003, http://animaldiversity.org/accounts/Oncorhynchus_tshawytscha/

4. C. J. Cederholm, et al., "Pacific Salmon and Wildlife: Ecological Contexts, Relationships, and Implications for Management," Washington Department of Fish and Wildlife, 2000, http://wdfw.wa.gov/publications/00063/wdfw00063.pdf

5. T. E. Reimchen, et al., "Isotopic Evidence for Enrichment of Salmon-Derived Nutrients in Vegetation, Soil, and Insects in Riparian Zones in Coastal British Columbia," American Fisheries Society, 2002, http://web.uvic.ca/~reimlab/n15clayoquot.pdf

6. Hitoshi Araki, et al., "Fitness of Hatchery-Reared Salmonids in the Wild," *Evolutionary Applications*, May 2008, pp. 342-355, http://www.ncbi.nlm.nih.gov/pmc/articles/PMC3352433/

7. Nathan F. Putman, et al., "An Inherited Magnetic Map Guides Ocean Navigation in Juvenile Pacific Salmon," *Current Biology*, February 17, 2014, http://www.dfw.state.or.us/fish/OHRC/docs/2014/Putman%20inherited%20salmon%20map.pdf

WORKS CONSULTED

Araki, Hitoshi, Barry A. Berejikian, Michael J. Ford, and Michael S. Blouin. "Fitness of Hatchery-Reared Salmonids in the Wild." *Evolutionary Applications*, May 2008, pp. 342-355. http://www.ncbi.nlm.nih.gov/pmc/articles/PMC3352433/

Cederholm, C. J., D. H. Johnson, R. E. Bilby, L. G. Dominguez, A. M. Garrett, W. H. Graeber, E. L. Greda, M. D. Kunze, B. G. Marcot, J. F. Palmisano, R. W. Plotnikoff, W. G. Pearcy, C. A. Simenstad, and P. C. Trotter. "Pacific Salmon and Wildlife: Ecological Contexts, Relationships, and Implications for Management." Washington Department of Fish and Wildlife, 2000. http://wdfw.wa.gov/publications/00063/wdfw00063.pdf

Cincinnati Zoo. "American Alligator." September 4, 2012. http://cincinnatizoo.org/wp-content/uploads/2013/03/American-Alligator-In-Progress.pdf

Crandall, Keith A., and Jennifer E. Buhay. "Global Diversity of Crayfish (Astacidae, Cambaridae, and Parastacidae—Decapoda) in Freshwater." *Hydrobiologia*, January 1, 2008, pp. 295-301. http://decapoda.nhm.org/pdfs/27696/27696.pdf

Defenders of Wildlife. "American Alligator: Threats To American Alligators." http://www.defenders.org/american-alligator/threats

Delaney, Kevin. "Chinook Salmon." Alaska Department of Fish & Game, 2008. http://www.adfg.alaska.gov/static/education/wns/chinook_salmon.pdf

Ferry, David. "Leave It to Beavers." *Atlantic*, May 21, 2012. http://theatlantic.com/magazine/archive/2012/06/leave-it-to-beavers/308980

Gherardi, F. "Towards a Sustainable Human Use of Freshwater Crayfish (Crustacea, Decapoda, Astacidea)." *Knowledge and Management of Aquatic Ecosystems*, issue 401, 2011. http://www.kmae-journal.org/articles/kmae/pdf/2011/02/kmae110008.pdf

Gin, Kevin. "*Notophthalmus viridescens*." AmphibiaWeb, November 25, 2003. http://amphibiaweb.org/cgi/amphib_query?where-genus=Notophthalmus&where-species=viridescens&account=amphibiaweb

Haemig, Paul D. "Ecology of the Beaver." *Ecology Online Sweden*, 2012. http://www.ecology.info/beaver-ecology.htm

Heter, Elmo W. "Transplanting Beavers by Airplane and Parachute." *Journal of Wildlife Management*, April 1950, pp. 143-147. http://www.martinezbeavers.org/wordpress/wp-content/uploads/2012/05/airdrop-STUDY-beaver.pdf

Idaho Rivers United. "About Salmon: Nutrients from Salmon." http://www.idahorivers.org/protectsalmon/about.aspx?page=nutrients

Jackson, Scott, and Thomas Decker. "Beavers in Massachusetts." University of Massachusetts Cooperative Extension System, Massachusetts Division of Fisheries and Wildlife. http://www.bio.umass.edu/biology/conn.river/beaver.html

Loughman, Zachary. "Crayfish." *e-WV: The West Virginia Encyclopedia*, August 1, 2014. http://www.wvencyclopedia.org/articles/2426

Magoulick, Daniel D. "Invasive Species Effects, Population Status and Population Genetics of Crayfish Species of Greatest Conservation Need (*Orconectes marchandi, Orconectes eupunctus,* and *Cambarus hubbsi*) in the Ozark Highlands of Arkansas and Missouri," Arkansas Wildlife Action Plan, 2014. http://www.wildlifearkansas.com/proposals/2014Preproposals/Preproposals2014.html

Mason, Jim. "Beaver." Great Plains Nature Center. http://www.gpnc.org/beaver.htm

Michigan Department of Natural Resources. "Fish Ladders and Weirs." http://www.michigan.gov/dnr/0,4570,7-153-10364_19092-46291--,00.html

Müller-Schwarze, Dietland. *The Beaver: Its Life and Impact*, Second Edition. Ithaca, NY: Cornell University Press, 2011.

National Park Service. "American Crocodile: Species Profile." Everglades National Park, Florida. http://www.nps.gov/ever/naturescience/crocodile.htm

National Park Service Natural Sounds Program. "American Alligator: In Depth." Everglades National Park, Florida, August 24, 2008. http://www.nps.gov/ever/naturescience/alligatorindepth.htm

National Wildlife Federation. "Chinook Salmon." http://www.nwf.org/wildlife/wildlife-library/amphibians-reptiles-and-fish/chinook-salmon.aspx

New Hampshire Public Television. "American Alligator—*Alligator Mississippiensis*." *NatureWorks*. http://www.nhptv.org/natureworks/americanalligator.htm

New Hampshire Public Television. "Beaver—*Castor canadensis*." *NatureWorks*. http://www.nhptv.org/natureworks/beaver.htm

Nifong, James C., R. L. Nifong, B. R. Silliman, R. H. Lowers, L. J. Guillette, Jr., J. M. Ferguson, M. Welsh, K. Abernathy, and G.

WORKS CONSULTED

Marshall. "Animal-Borne Imaging Reveals Novel Insights into the Foraging Behaviors and Diel Activity of a Large-Bodied Apex Predator, the American Alligator (*Alligator mississippiensis*)." *PLOS One*, 2014. http://www.ncbi.nlm.nih.gov/pmc/articles/PMC3893291/

NOAA Fisheries. "Chinook Salmon (*Oncorhynchus tshawytscha*)." January 21, 2015. http://www.nmfs.noaa.gov/pr/species/fish/chinooksalmon.htm

NOAA Fisheries. "What is Scientific Classification?" National Marine Mammal Laboratory, Marine Mammal Education Web. http://www.afsc.noaa.gov/nmml/education/taxonomy.php

Oregon Sea Grant. "Species at a Glance: Crayfish." *Aquatic Invasions! A Menace to the West.* http://seagrant.oregonstate.edu/sites/default/files/invasive-species/toolkit/crayfish.pdf

Pajerski, Lauren, Benjamin Schechter, and Robin Street. "*Alligator mississippiensis*." *Animal Diversity Web*, October 4, 2000. http://animaldiversity.org/accounts/Alligator_mississippiensis/

Parks & Wildlife Service, Tasmania. "Giant Freshwater Crayfish (*Astacopsis gouldi*)." November 28, 2011. http://www.parks.tas.gov.au/indeX.aspX?base=11213

Pflieger, William. *The Crayfishes of Missouri.* Jefferson City, MO: Missouri Department of Conservation, 1996.

Putman, Nathan F., Michelle M. Scanlan, Eric J. Billman, Joseph P. O'Neil, Ryan B. Couture, Thomas P. Quinn, Kenneth J. Lohmann, and David L. G. Noakes. "An Inherited Magnetic Map Guides Ocean Navigation in Juvenile Pacific Salmon." *Current Biology*, February 17, 2014. http://www.dfw.state.or.us/fish/OHRC/docs/2014/Putman%20inherited%20salmon%20map.pdf

Reimchen, T. E., D. Mathewson, M. D. Hocking, J. Moran, and D. Harris. "Isotopic Evidence for Enrichment of Salmon-Derived Nutrients in Vegetation, Soil, and Insects in Riparian Zones in Coastal British Columbia." American Fisheries Society, 2002. http://web.uvic.ca/~reimlab/n15clayoquot.pdf

Riemland, Shannon. "*Notophthalmus viridescens*, Eastern Newt." University of Michigan Museum of Zoology, *Animal Diversity Web*, October 4, 2000. http://animaldiversity.org/accounts/Notophthalmus_viridescens/

Saalfeld, David T., Warren C. Conway, and Gary E. Calkins. "Food Habits of American Alligators (*Alligator mississippiensis*) in East Texas." *Southeastern Naturalist*, December 2011, pp. 659-672.

Santucci, Vincent L., and Lindsay McClelland, editors. *National Park Service Paleontological Research*, Volume 2. Denver, CO: National Park Service, 1995. http://www.nature.nps.gov/geology/paleontology/Publications/research_volumes/nps_paleo_vol2/research%20volume%202_paleo.pdf

Scott, Caren. "*Oncorhynchus tshawytscha*: Blackmouth." University of Michigan Museum of Zoology, *Animal Diversity Web*, June 2, 2003. http://animaldiversity.org/accounts/Oncorhynchus_tshawytscha/

US Fish & Wildlife Service. "American Alligator: *Alligator mississippiensis*." February 2008. http://www.fws.gov/endangered/esa-library/pdf/alligator.pdf

FURTHER READING

Feigenbaum, Aaron. *American Alligators: Freshwater Survivors* (America's Animal Comebacks). New York: Bearport Publishing Company, 2008.

Goldish, Meish. *Little Newts*. New York: Bearport Publishing Company, 2010.

Kalman, Bobbie. *The Life Cycle of a Beaver*. New York: Crabtree Publishing Co., 2007.

Kalman, Bobbie. *The Life Cycle of a Crayfish*. New York: Crabtree Publishing Co., 2007.

Miller, Debbie S., and John H. Eiler. *A King Salmon Journey*. Fairbanks, AK: University of Alaska Press, 2014.

ON THE INTERNET

Animal Planet, Fooled by Nature: Beaver Dams https://www.youtube.com/watch?v=Na2HYq11yuM

Crayfish Habitat, Food, Trapping, & Aquariums http://crayfishfacts.org/

National Geographic Kids: American Alligator http://kids.nationalgeographic.com/content/kids/en_US/animals/american-alligator/

PBS, DragonflyTV: Salmon by Andy, Mason, and Marshall http://pbskids.org/dragonflytv/show/salmonrun.html

GLOSSARY

apex predator (EY-peks PRED-uh-ter)—a predator at the top of its food chain, having no predators

cache (kash)—a hiding place, especially on the ground, or that which is hidden in it

compete (kuhm-PEET)—to struggle against another for something, such as food or shelter

conservationist (kon-ser-VEY-shuh-nist)—a person who works to protect and restore natural resources like animals, plants, streams, and oceans

crustacean (kruh-STEY-shuhn)—a member of a species that lives in water and has a hard shell, like a lobster, shrimp, crab, or crayfish

diameter (dahy-AM-i-ter)—the length of a straight line passing from side to side through the center of a circle, like a tree trunk

ecosystem (EE-koh-sis-tuhm)—a system of interaction of the plants and animals in a community

engineer (en-juh-NEER)—a person or animal skilled in the design or construction of something

exoskeleton (ek-soh-SKEL-i-tuhn)—a hard shell on the outside of an animal

fertilize (FUR-tuhl-ahyz)—to bring together the male sperm and the female egg to develop into offspring

gland—an organ that produces a substance, usually a liquid

habitat (HAB-i-tat)—the place where a plant or animal naturally lives and grows

incubate (IN-kyuh-beyt)—to develop or grow in preparation for hatching

instinct (IN-stingkt)—a behavior or activity that an animal does naturally, without learning how to do it

invertebrate (in-VUR-tuh-brit)—an animal without a backbone

larvae (LAHR-vuh)—the young of an invertebrate animal

litter (LIT-er)—a group of babies that an animal has at the same birth

magnetic field (mag-NET-ik)—an area in which a magnetic force can affect other magnets or electric currents

metamorphose (met-uh-MAWR-fohz)—to change the form of something

native (NEY-tiv)—currently living in the place where it originally lived (as in a species of plant or animal)

navigate (NAV-i-geyt)—to move over land or water with a specific direction

order—a major subdivision of a class of living things

plankton (PLANGK-tuhn)—tiny organisms that live in water; usually floating near the surface

poaching (POH-ching)—hunting animals illegally

pupil (PYOO-puhl)—the small dark center of an eye

range (reynj)—the physical area within which animals of a certain species can be found

sediment (SED-uh-muhnt)—matter that has settled at the bottom of a liquid

snout—the part of an animal that contains its nose and jaws

spawn—to place a mass of eggs or sperm directly into the water

sperm (spurm)—a male reproductive cell

stressful (STRES-fuhl)—causing strain or discomfort for a person, animal, or plant

transition (tran-ZISH-uhn)—movement from one stage to another

waterproof (WAW-ter-proof)—not allowing water to pass through

wean (ween)—to feed a baby solid food until it no longer needs its mother's milk

INDEX

About the Author

Bonnie Hinman has loved studying nature since she was a child growing up on her family's farm. Today she is a certified Missouri Master Naturalist and works in her community educating children and adults about the natural world around them. She also volunteers her time to restore and maintain the local ecosystem. Hinman has had more than thirty books published including Mitchell Lane's *Threat to the Leatherback Turtle*. She lives with her husband Bill in Joplin, Missouri, near her children and five grandchildren.